SCIENCE OF THE SUMMER OLYMPICS

EDGE BOOKS

THE SCIENCE BEHIND SWIMMING, DIVING AND OTHER WATER SPORTS

by Amanda Lanser

raintree
a Capstone company — publishers for children

Raintree is an imprint of Capstone Global Library Limited, a company incorporated in England and Wales having its registered office at 264 Banbury Road, Oxford, OX2 7DY – Registered company number: 6695582

www.raintree.co.uk
myorders@raintree.co.uk

ISBN 978 1 4747 1140 1 (hardback)   978 1 4747 1144 9 (paperback)
19 18 17 16 15   21 20 19 18 17
10 9 8 7 6 5 4 3 2 1   10 9 8 7 6 5 4 3 2 1

British Library Cataloguing in Publication Data
A full catalogue record for this book is available from the British Library.

Editorial Credits
Arnold Ringstad, editor
Craig Hinton, designer
Laura Polzin, production specialist

Photo Credits
AP Images: Alastair Grant, 7, David J. Phillip, 26, Julio Cortez, 25, Kirsty Wigglesworth, 29, Koji Sasahara, 20 (right), Mark Allan, 1, 16, 21, Mark J. Terrill, 4, 10–11, 20 (background), Matt Dunham, 28, Michael Sohn, 20 (left); Dorling Kindersley, 8–9 (top); Dorling Kindersley/Thinkstock, 8–9 (middle top), 8–9 (middle bottom), 8–9 (bottom); Getty Images: Adek Berry/AFP, 22, Al Bello, 18, Jamie Squire, 19, Tim Clary/AFP, 14–15; iStockphoto: cmcderm1, 24, IPGGutenbergUKLtd, 12–13, microgen, 6; Nejron Photo/Shutterstock Images, cover

We would like to thank Mark Walsh, Associate Professor of Exercise Science at Miami University, Oxford, Ohio, for his help in the preparation of this book.

CONTENTS

Missy Franklin reaches for the wall at the end of her record-setting 200-metre backstroke race in the 2012 Olympics.

CHAPTER 1

SWIMMING
WITH SCIENCE

Missy Franklin had a reason to smile. The 17-year-old swimmer from the United States had just broken a world record. She swam the 200-metre backstroke event in 2 minutes, 4.06 seconds. Her time was nearly a second faster than the previous record. Before the 2012 London Olympic Games were over, she would earn four gold medals and break another world record.

Like all **aquatic** Olympic athletes, Franklin used science to her advantage. **Gravity, buoyancy**, psychology and other scientific topics come into play for athletes who want to reach the medal podium.

aquatic having to do with water
gravity force that causes objects to move towards Earth's centre
buoyancy ability to float

○○○○○

Swimming science

The summer Olympic Games include four aquatic events. Athletes compete in swimming, diving, water polo and synchronized swimming. Some of these events involve short bursts of energy, while others require endurance. All of them test competitors' skills.

Athletes use biology, **biomechanics**, physics, **hydrodynamics** and psychology to pull ahead of the pack. They study physics concepts such as **drag** and **thrust**. They learn how lung capacity and flexibility affect their swimming. Coaches and athletes study how the mind affects performance. Athletes focus their minds and energy on doing their best.

biomechanics study of how forces act on a living body
hydrodynamics study of the forces that affect or are exerted by water
drag force that slows down a swimmer's body as it moves through the water
thrust force produced by a swimmer's arm movement, similar to an aeroplane propeller

Athletes in the water polo event must build up their strength and endurance.

Swimming event history

Swimming events were not part of the ancient Olympics. But they have always been a part of the modern Olympics. Freestyle events were part of the first modern Olympics in 1896. Other strokes were added later. Water polo was added as a sport in 1900. Diving was added in 1904. At first, only men competed in swimming events. In 1912 female swimmers were allowed to compete. Synchronized swimming made its debut in 1984.

SWIMMING STROKES

Body should rotate only 30–40 degrees to each side.

Hips should be held as high as possible to reduce drag.

breath phase

breaststroke

A stroke in which arms move together and feet move together. The arms make a heart-shaped pattern. The kick resembles that of a frog.

butterfly

A stroke in which arms move together to make a keyhole shape. The trunk and legs move together in a dolphin kick.

freestyle

The name of an event in which a swimmer can use any stroke. Almost all swimmers use a crawl stroke. It is the fastest of the swimming strokes. The arms alternate stroking over the surface of the water. The feet flutter kick.

backstroke

A stroke performed on a swimmer's back. Swimmers alternate arms stroking through the water and use a flutter kick.

kick

After kicking, the swimmer glides forwards for a moment, carried by her **inertia**.

glide phase

The swimmer may take a breath every stroke or every other stroke, depending on how much oxygen his body needs at that point in the race.

inertia body's tendency to remain still, or to continue moving at the same speed in the same direction

A Japanese synchronized swimming duo competes in the 2012 London Olympics. Swimming athletes deal with forces unlike those faced by athletes on land.

CHAPTER 2

FORCES ON
SWIMMERS

Aquatic Olympic sports are different from any others. When swimming, athletes' bodies are horizontal in the water, rather than vertical as on land. Water moves differently from air. Athletes make little or no contact with the ground. These conditions make performing in the water challenging. Aquatic athletes must adapt to them.

Gravity versus buoyancy

Buoyancy is an upward **force** that water puts on an athlete's body. Gravity is the opposite force. It pulls an athlete down toward the centre of Earth – in this case, the bottom of the pool.

Staying horizontal requires a balance between buoyancy and gravity. Swimmers' lungs do more than just allow the athletes to breathe. They also help the swimmers float. Body fat is naturally buoyant too, and it helps swimmers stay afloat.

force push or pull that changes the speed or direction of a body or object

drag

Drag slows the swimmer's forward movement through the water. This force is generated by the water ahead of the swimmer pushing against her movement.

thrust

Thrust pushes the swimmer forwards through the water. This force is generated by the swimmer moving her arms and legs to push against the water.

Force, thrust, lift and resistance

All athletes use force to gain speed. Runners push against the ground to create force. Swimmers only push off a hard surface at the start of their race and when turning at the end of the pool. When moving through the water, they create speed in other ways.

Swimmers use their arms and legs to produce thrust. This force moves them through the water. When they push back against the water with their limbs, the result is an equal and opposite force that pushes them forwards. Kicks and arm strokes also create **lift**.

lift force on an object perpendicular to that object's motion

buoyancy

Buoyancy pulls the swimmer upwards towards the surface of the water. This force is generated by the swimmer's lower **density** compared to the water.

gravity

Gravity pulls the swimmer down towards the centre of Earth. This force is generated by Earth's mass.

density amount of mass an object has, divided by its volume

The Thorpedo

Ian Thorpe is nicknamed "the Thorpedo." He is a retired Australian swimmer. He won five gold medals at the 2000 and 2004 Olympic Games. Standing 1.96 metres (6 feet, 5 inches) tall and weighing 104 kilograms (229 pounds), Thorpe needed to **accelerate** his large mass through the water. Strength training helped him produce a lot of force.

accelerate to change in speed or direction

Creating thrust and lift helps swimmers battle the effects of drag. Drag is the effect of water pushing back on the swimmer, slowing him or her down. Keeping the body straight and horizontal in the water reduces drag. This allows the swimmer to have less surface area facing forwards. It lets her or him slip through the water more efficiently.

Ian Thorpe leaps into the water at the start of a race in the 2004 Athens Olympics.

Tom Daley dives during the 10-metre platform event in the 2012 London Olympics.

CHAPTER 3

THE DYNAMICS
OF DIVING

British diver Tom Daley was just 14 years old when he became an Olympian at the 2008 Beijing Games. Daley was among the youngest divers ever to compete in the Olympics. He competed in the 10-metre platform and 10-metre synchro diving events at Beijing, and again in London in 2012. After a disappointing performance in the qualifying rounds, Daley turned it around and took the bronze in the 10-metre platform in London at the age of 18. He tucked, twisted and somersaulted through four high-scoring dives to earn his place on the medal podium. Science was there helping him all along the way. From the takeoff to the spins and flips of the diving poses to the perfect entry into the water, the laws of physics play a critical role in a medal-winning dive performance.

PLATFORMS AND
SPRINGBOARDS

springboard

A diving springboard is flexible. Moving the flexible end of the board by jumping on it stores energy in the board. Divers jump in time with the board so the board's energy is transferred to them before they jump off.

Takeoff!

Divers need to create force to propel their bodies through the air while performing a combination of moves that make up a dive routine. To create force, divers push off a diving board or platform. British scientist Sir Isaac Newton's third law of motion says the upward force will be equal to the downward force divers put against the board. In other words, the harder they jump, the higher they go. The higher they go, the more time they have in midair to complete their dive routines.

All the force needed to rotate, somersault, twist and spin comes from the takeoff. In addition to jumping high into the air, takeoffs must allow divers to clear the diving board on the way down. That means they cannot jump straight up. They must jump at an angle that will let them fall past the board into the water.

tuck

The diver's body is bent at the waist and knees. The thighs touch the chest and the toes are pointed. In this position the diver's mass is as close to the point of rotation as possible, maximizing rotational speed.

Divers and their coaches create dives from three main poses: pikes, straights and tucks. From there they add rotation, twists and spins. Judges score divers on their approaches to the edge of the diving board, their takeoffs, their execution of their poses and their entries into the water. As soon as a diver leaves the platform or springboard, his or her angular momentum remains constant. However, changing poses can change the distribution of the diver's mass, increasing or decreasing rotational speed.

pike

The diver bends at the waist and the legs are straight. The diver's mass moves closer to the point of rotation, increasing rotational speed.

Divers work to present as little surface area to the water as possible during their entries. This ensures a smooth, perfect finish to their dives.

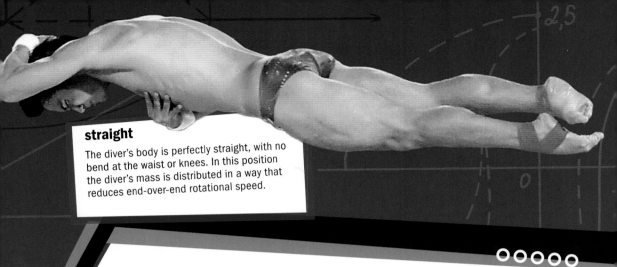

straight
The diver's body is perfectly straight, with no bend at the waist or knees. In this position the diver's mass is distributed in a way that reduces end-over-end rotational speed.

Rotate, twist, spin

Once divers leave the board, gravity is the only force acting on them as they fly through air. The force they generate off the board must be enough for them to complete their dive routines before gravity pulls them towards the water's surface.

Entry

A diver's entry into the water is the final part of the dive. In Olympic competition, divers get more points if their entries have little or no splash. This entry is called a rip entry. When performed correctly, it creates a sound like paper ripping. Divers work to be perfectly straight when they enter the water, with their hands clasped above their heads. The straighter a diver enters the water, the less his or her body impacts the water's surface. This means a smaller area of water is disturbed by the entry. After the diver's hands break the water's surface, the rest of his or her body follows him or her through the same part of the water. The result is a smaller splash.

Maggie Steffens tosses the ball over her opponents in a match during the 2012 London Olympics.

CHAPTER 4

THE SCIENCE OF
WATER POLO

Maggie Steffens scored five of the eight goals for the United States in the gold-medal water polo game at the London Olympics in 2012. She and her teammates won 8–5 over Spain to earn the gold in one of the Olympics' most demanding sports. As in swimming and diving, science is at work in this thrilling event.

What is water polo?

Water polo is typically played in a pool measuring about 30 metres (100 feet) by 20 metres (66 feet). The pool is divided in half, and each end has a goal that is 3 metres (10 feet) wide. Teams have seven players each, including one goalkeeper per side. Players try to throw the ball past the goalkeeper into the other team's goal.

Creating thrust

Like competitive swimmers, water polo players must create thrust to move through the water. But this is even more of a challenge for polo players. Swimmers can create force and momentum when they perform a flip turn. Polo players rarely make contact with the side or bottom of the pool.

The third law of motion helps explain how water polo players stay afloat. When a swimmer's arms and legs push against the water, the water pushes back with equal force. Polo players use a technique called **sculling**. The pressure of their arms against the water creates lift. It helps the athletes stay afloat and in a vertical position. Water polo players also use a special eggbeater kick. It works in a way similar to sculling. It keeps swimmers' heads above the water while they are vertical in the pool.

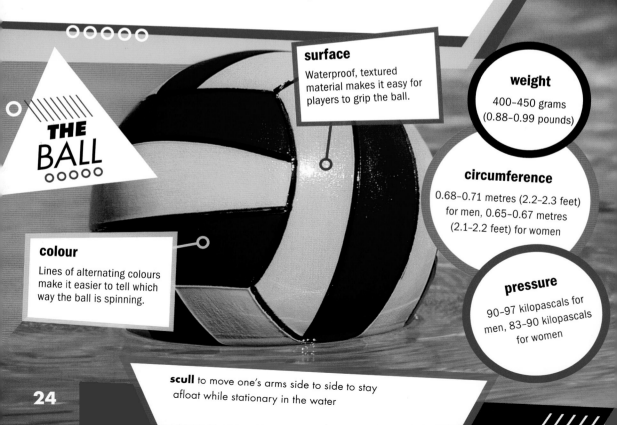

THE BALL

surface
Waterproof, textured material makes it easy for players to grip the ball.

weight
400–450 grams (0.88–0.99 pounds)

circumference
0.68–0.71 metres (2.2–2.3 feet) for men, 0.65–0.67 metres (2.1–2.2 feet) for women

colour
Lines of alternating colours make it easier to tell which way the ball is spinning.

pressure
90–97 kilopascals for men, 83–90 kilopascals for women

scull to move one's arms side to side to stay afloat while stationary in the water

Most shot speed comes from:

» body rotation (30–35 percent)

» shoulder rotation (20–30 percent)

» elbow extension (22–27 percent)

» wrist extension (8–13 percent)

The time from the furthest part of the swing to the ball release should be about 0.17 seconds. This can lead to throwing speeds of up to 80 kilometres (50 miles) per hour. Faster shots are more likely to score goals, since the goalie has less time to react.

Players rise as far out of the water as possible. Air has much less resistance than water, so getting as much of their motion done in the air as possible leads to faster throws.

When players are swinging their arms back to throw, at the furthest part of the swing their shoulders should line up with the goal. This will let them put the full force of the body's rotation into the shot.

Rebecca Adlington enters the water during a race in the 2012 London Olympics.

CHAPTER 5

TRAINING AND **TECHNOLOGY**

Before she retired in 2013, Rebecca Adlington was the UK's most successful swimmer. She swam the 400-metre freestyle and 800-metre freestyle at the 2008 Olympic Games. She broke world records and won two gold medals. She earned two bronze medals in those events in the 2012 Olympic Games. She is the most decorated British swimmer since 1908.

Today Adlington uses her experience and expertise to teach Olympic hopefuls. She supports them through hard training. She knows how difficult it can be to come back from a training session in which you do not reach your goals. Adlington understands the pressure these athletes face as they train for the Olympics. She knows psychology plays a role in the success of Olympic athletes.

US diver Katie Bell used music as part of her preparation at the London Olympics.

○○○○○

Mental and physical training

Mental training is part of an Olympic athlete's preparation. Developing an ideal mind-set is one aspect of mental training. Swimmers identify what mind-set they were in before and during their best performances. They use this information to create a repeatable mind-set. They may listen to music or go through the same routine before competing. They may pump themselves up or relax. With the right mind-set, they can reduce mistakes and focus their energy.

Whatever their sport, Olympic competitors must be strong. Aquatic athletes train in and out of the pool to build muscle. Muscle helps them create force, power, explosiveness and stability. Creating force helps swimmers move quickly through the water. Powerful swimmers can perform strokes over and over again until the end of the race.

Cutting-edge swimming gear

Science helps improve athletes' performance in the water. It also helps companies develop state-of-the-art equipment. Specialized swimsuits can cut down on drag and reduce times. In some cases, these suits can provide such an advantage that they are banned from competitions.

Whether they race through the water, dive from great heights or hurl a buoyant ball through a goal, all aquatic athletes use science in some way. From the psychology of training to the physical forces of competition, they rely on scientific principles to win Olympic medals.

the LZR Racer

Low-profile zipper and welded seams reduce drag.

Layers of lightweight fabric trap air, making swimmers more buoyant.

Sturdy, firm panels allow the suit to help stabilize the swimmer's core.

Suit covers more of a swimmer's body than other suits, including the legs and trunk, reducing drag from the skin.

HIGH-TECH SUITS

Swimwear company Speedo made waves in the 2008 Olympics. Its new suit was developed with the help of NASA scientists. Ninety-eight percent of swimmers who earned medals were wearing the LZR Racer suit. So were the swimmers who broke 23 of the 25 world records smashed at the Beijing Olympics.

In 2010 the LZR Racer was banned from future Olympics. Officials believed the suit gave swimmers too much of an advantage. But Speedo continued its research. In the 2012 Olympic Games, new LZR Racer X suits made their debut. The suits come down to swimmers' knees, not their ankles.

GLOSSARY

accelerate to change in speed or direction

aquatic having to do with water

biomechanics study of how forces act on a living body

buoyancy ability to float

density amount of mass an object has, divided by its volume

drag force that slows down a swimmer's body as it moves through the water

force push or pull that changes the speed or direction of a body or object

gravity force that causes objects to move towards Earth's centre

hydrodynamics study of the forces that affect or are exerted by water

inertia body's tendency to remain still, or to continue moving at the same speed in the same direction

lift force on an object perpendicular to that object's motion

scull to move one's arms side to side to stay afloat while stationary in the water

thrust force produced by a swimmer's arm movement, similar to an aeroplane propeller

READ MORE

All About the Olympics, Nick Hunter (Raintree, 2012).

Swimming and Diving (Summer Olympic Sports), Allan Morey (Amicus, 2015).

The Olympics: Going for Gold: A Guide to the Summer Games, Joe Fullman (Wayland, 2015).

COMPREHENSION QUESTIONS

1. Take a look at the diving pose diagrams on pages 20–21. Which pose would a diver want to use just before entering the water? Which one has the best chance of becoming a rip entry? Why?

2. Think about the high-tech swimsuits discussed in Chapter 5. Do you agree with the decision to ban these swimsuits? State the reasons for your opinion.

WEBSITES

BBC: Diving
http://www.bbc.com/sport/olympics/2012/sports/diving
Learn more about the diving events and medalists from the 2012 London Olympics.

BBC: Swimming
http://www.bbc.com/sport/olympics/2012/sports/swimming
Read about the top winners in swimming competitions at the 2012 London Olympics.

British Swimming
http://www.swimming.org/britishswimming
Explore the official online home of the national governing body for aquatic sports.

INDEX